"Thinking Hebraically is a small book with a l will bless you and will inexorably draw you into time you spend reading through it the first time wui wnei your appeine, muking you want more of the same. It will also make you go back to this book to refresh your memory, thinking, "Did he really say that?

"The nuggets revealed will draw you time and again to revel in each revelation, so you will look forward to each book that Alyosha writes. ENJOY THIS OPENING OF SCRIPTURE, A PICTURE OF BLESSINGS TO COME!"

BILL MORFORD
Author
American Bible Translator
Hebraic Specialist and Bible Teacher

"There is no doubt in my mind or in my heart that Alyosha Ryabinov has shared the very Chokmah (divine wisdom) of the Almighty as His Spirit revealed His resplendent mysteries in each captivating chapter. Every Hebrew word exploded with rich meaning and substance. Truly, this book is a powerhouse of revelation."

DR. VICTORIA SARVADI
Author, *Just a Little Girl*
Founder, The Nathaniel Foundation and victoriasarvadi.com

"A very enjoyable read, full of colorful explanations. The author's use of the Hebrew language will be helpful to readers. His story, as relayed in the introduction, gives us his motivation for writing, and the remainder of his book strongly reflect his love for God and for the Jewish roots of the Bible. Alyosha writes with deep passion and conviction in the desire to draw his readers to better understand who God is, as well as who they themselves are. His emphasis on the relational nature of God throughout the book is encouraging."

RABBI DR. D. FRIEDMAN
Former Academic Dean, King of Kings College
Jerusalem, Israel

Thinking Hebraically

Uncovering "Nuggets" in the Bible Through A Hebrew Mindset

ALYOSHA RYABINOV

with the help of
LONNIE LANE

STOREHOUSE MEDIA GROUP, LLC
JACKSONVILLE, FLORIDA

THINKING HEBRAICALLY: *Uncovering "Nuggets" in the Bible through a Hebrew Mindset*

Storehouse Media Group, LLC
Jacksonville, Florida
www.StorehouseMediaGroup.com
publish@StorehouseMediaGroup.com

Ordering Information:
Quantity sales. Special discounts are available with the Publisher at the email address above and type in subject line "Special Sales Department."

The views expressed in this work are solely those of the author(s) and do not necessarily reflect the views of the publisher, and the publisher hereby disclaims any responsibility for them.

Cover Design by Gwenn Danae

Thinking Hebraically / Alyosha Ryabinov with the Help of Lonnie Lane— 1st ed.

ISBN-13: 978-1-943106-18-9 (paperback)
ISBN-13: 978-1-943106-19-6 (ebook)

Library of Congress Control Number: 2017962725

Printed in the United States of America

DEDICATION

Dedicated to my loving wife, Jody, for her support and encouragement
as well as taking many duties upon herself to give me time
to complete this book.

I also want to dedicate this book to my children, Josiah and Yasmine,
as well as to all the grandchildren: the existing ones
and those who are yet to come.

ACKNOWLEDGMENTS

I want to express my thanks to the following special people who gave of their time freely to help me write this book: Lonnie Lane for transcribing and editing and Alexandra Wolf for editing and translating this book into German. And many thanks also to Jane Bakewell for her help in editing.

CONTENTS

INTRODUCTION

We live in days when God is restoring what must be restored before Yeshua (Jesus) will return. Peter, in his first message at *Shavuot* (Pentecost) declared, "Repent…and turn to God that your sins may be blotted out, so that times of refreshing may come from the presence of the Lord, and that He may send Messiah Yeshua, who was preached to you before, whom heaven must receive until the times of restoration of all things, which God has spoken by the mouth of all His holy prophets since the world began" (Acts 3:19-21).

God is restoring much today. We will be discussing some of those things. Primarily He is restoring the foundation, which is rooted in our forefathers. Isaiah 51:1, 2 says, "Listen to Me, you who follow after (or pursue) righteousness, you who seek the Lord. Look to the rock from which you were hewn…. Look to Abraham your father and Sarah who bore you." So Abraham and Sarah are the father and mother to whom we are to look. That means, in the Lord we have a father and a mother. Isaiah is speaking to those "who follow after righteousness." If you wish to follow after righteousness, that applies to you.

The Scriptures say to honor your mother and father so that things will go well for you (Exodus 20:12). Many believers teach about curses passing from generation to generation, even curses from the fathers passing to third and fourth generations. But not many people talk about the blessings of generations, even back to the blessings of the forefathers.

My personal story relating to the blessings of the forefathers began in 1998 with a strong desire to begin looking into Hebrew. I was born and raised in the Soviet Union – primarily a god-less country. Even though I was Jewish, I had no typical Jewish upbringing and was estranged from the tenets of Judaism. I met the Lord shortly after immigrating to USA and from that point on my life took another direction and I found myself on a road to discovery of my Hebraic (Jewish) heritage. In 1998 I was in Israel for a visit, and I felt the Lord wanted me to buy a Hebrew English Bible and begin to read it. I did not have a lot of knowledge of Hebrew at that time. It took me about three years just to read through the Torah, the first five books of Moses.

Then I started to reread it again, and a whole new world began to open up that I had not seen before. Amazing pictures and patterns began to emerge on the pages. I had not seen these reading the Bible in either English or Russian, which is my mother tongue, having been born in Ukraine. Then in 2005 I was in Israel again and at a Messianic service where familiar songs were being sung in three languages; English, Russian and Hebrew. By this time, I understood all three languages. When sung in Russian and English, the songs were very nice and they were special, but when they were sung in Hebrew, I wanted to cry. So I began to wonder, what is it about this Hebrew language that is different from all the other languages?

Then the Lord began to explain it to me. He told me, "It is time for you to understand why it is in your heart to learn the Hebrew language. If you think the reason is so you can read the Scriptures and understand, that is a good reason, but it is not the main reason. One day you will live in Israel, but it is still not the main reason. The main reason is that what has been cut off from your forefathers is being restored to you." I began to understand that the work of the enemy has been to cut off that which was built by the forefathers but in which we today must learn to stand. The blessings of the forefathers must pass from generation to generation. God wanted to reconnect me to the former generations, all the way back to the forefathers – meaning to Abraham, Isaac and Jacob. Through them God built a foundation upon which everything else stands. He told me, "If you do not stand on that foundation, you will not fulfill your purpose and calling." I offer you these insights with the hope that they will help you to fulfill your own calling in the Lord through His truths.

Chapter

1   Restoration

I believe that every generation builds upon the foundation of the previous generations. In every generation God releases a new revelation. But it must be built upon the previous revelation in truth. After the patriarchs came Moses, then Joshua, then the prophets, kings, etc. It all climaxed in Yeshua. Even in my personal call, in order for me to fulfill what God has for me, I must be connected to those who went before me. The Scriptures specifically say we are to honor our mother and our father lest our days be cut short (Exodus 20:12). This extends back to Abraham and Sarah who were our foundational parents. Part of the restoration is that we must look to Abraham our father and Sarah who bore us (Isaiah 51:1, 2).

So let us talk about Abraham. Who was he? The Scriptures say he was a Hebrew. There are two reasons why he was called a Hebrew. One, he was a descendent of Eber (Genesis 10:24, 25) who was a descendent of Shem. The meaning of the name Eber in Hebrew means to cross over. When God spoke to Abram (before He later renamed him Abraham), He said, "Get out of your country, from your family, and from your father's house, to a land I will show you. I will make you a great nation; I will bless you and make your name great and you shall be a blessing" (Genesis 12:1, 2). So Abram listened to the voice of God, left Haran and went to the land of Canaan. He crossed over to the place that God destined for him.

The pattern here is that we leave the identity of the human family that carries generational curses and cross over to God, allowing God to become our Father. Then the Father will bless us and we become a blessing to others. That is the pattern. We will go more deeply into this as we go on.

We are talking about Hebraic foundations. Was Hebrew the mother tongue of all other languages? When we go to Genesis 11 we see that originally the whole world had the same language and speech. What was that one language? Genesis 10 gives us some background. It deals with the genealogies of the three sons of Noah. In the genealogy of Ham, we come to an interesting character named Nimrod. He was a grandson of Noah's son Ham. Nimrod is only mentioned three times in Scripture, yet he seemed to be a very significant character. It says he was a mighty one on the earth, so he obviously had a lot of earthly power and authority. It says, "He was a mighty hunter *before* the Lord" (Genesis 10:9). There are people who see these words in the positive, but it is not really so.

First of all, his name means "rebel" in Hebrew (The root word is *mered* – מרד). Names in Hebrew represent the character and call of a person, but there are more clues about who he was. In ancient times, the mighty leaders were portrayed in the act of hunting. It did not mean he actually had to hunt, but it describes someone who is powerful. Words in Hebrew can be either positive or negative depending on the context, on being able to see the bigger picture. The word "before" can mean before or against. Two armies face each other but they are against each other. The word before in Hebrew is לפני *(leef-nay)*. Also at the root of this word is the word פן *(pen)* – which means face. Scripture also says the beginning of Nimrod's kingdom was Babel, and he then added other cities. Basically, he built an empire. He built a kingdom at a time when there were no kingdoms on earth; God alone was king over the whole earth. But Nimrod started his own kingdom in the face of God – really in opposition to God.

The name of the very first city in Hebrew is *Bavel* – בבל (in English, Babel), which means confusion. So the beginning of his kingdom was based on confusion on earth. The fact that he thought he could successfully build his own empire against God's kingdom was part of his own confusion, for it certainly was not based on truth. Later on, the city of Babel is where God confused the languages. It happened in that first city. What happened is that people lost the ability to communicate, which brought great confusion on the earth.

Let us now look at the genealogy of another of Noah's sons, Shem (Genesis 10:21). Shem is the forefather of all the children of Eber, who was Shem's great-grandson. Here's a question: Why is this particular name emphasized when Shem had so many other children, grandchildren and great-grandchildren? Scripture says, "Shem is the father of Eber who was his great grandson." It means that name has an importance, which is why it is emphasized. When we look at Eber in verse 25 it says, "and to Eber were born two sons. The name of one was Peleg for in his days the earth was divided. His brother's name was Yoktan." This shows us a strange hint that brings up many questions.

We are told one son is Peleg and in his days the earth was divided, but no more information is given. The genealogy then continues not through him but through his brother Yoktan. It says nothing about Yoktan himself, but just continues the genealogy (vs. 26-29). Obviously, there is something significant there. So what can we find out about Peleg? His name means division, or a stream, a stream that is separated from the main body of water. Then we come to Chapter 11 where there is a description of the building of the Tower of Babel in the city of Babel and where the languages were confused. The Scriptures shift there again and repeat the genealogy of Shem again.

From verse 10 it says, "These are the generations of Shem." This genealogy focuses only on one of Shem's lineages, which goes through Eber and then to Peleg. His brother Yoktan is not even mentioned this time. Just the name Peleg (meaning separation or division) is mentioned. Even the genealogy got separated focusing on just one stream of names that led to Abram.

So what could have been the separation or division that was so significant? In Peleg's days the earth was divided. As we have seen his name means separation and division. And his genealogy was separated out from the rest of the people because only the direct ancestors and descendants of Peleg are mentioned. Everyone else is gone. The other genealogies deal with all the sons of Noah, everyone included, but in this genealogy, it deals only with one – Peleg. In understanding all the patterns of God, beginning with creation, He separates light from darkness. It is possible, then, that Peleg and his sons chose not to submit to the one world dark government of Nimrod and Babel and did not join Nimrod in building the tower. Therefore, his was quite possibly the only language that did not get confused.

Since this was the genealogy of Abraham who was Hebrew, he most likely spoke the ancient form of the language of Peleg. Could it be that the original language, which is mentioned in Genesis 11:1 was the Hebrew language? Before the separation of languages, it says, "Now the whole earth had one language and one speech." But it appears that this language did not get confused, or corrupted in the line of Abraham. The Hebrew sages believed that the ancient form of Hebrew was the mother tongue for all other languages.

Hebrew was the language of the patriarchs and the prophets, but when Israel was no longer in her land after the Roman exile, it was no longer used as a common language among the Jews. So for about 2000 years, Hebrew was not spoken except for prayers and reading

Tenakh.[1] Then about 100 years ago, as a fulfillment of the prophecy of Zephaniah 3:9, where it reads, "I will restore to the people a pure language, that they may call upon the name of YHWH, to serve him with one accord," part of the restoration of Israel to her land began with the restoration of Hebrew to the people. A "pure language" (*safa brura* – שפה ברורה) can also be translated as a clear language – one with no confusion. It is interesting that Hebrew does not have swear words. When Israelis get upset, they have to borrow expressions from other languages.

Every language, one way or another, reflects God somewhere. But Hebrew is the only language, which in its entirety reflects God, whether in its grammar, pictures, patterns, numbers, etc. There are so many aspects of this language that are clearly linked back to the beginning. I am not implying that everyone needs to learn Hebrew but laying a Hebraic foundation can revolutionize our lives. It is my heart's desire that people would understand their roots and true foundation in God.

If we continue the genealogy we come to Abraham. Since he too was a descendent of Eber, he was *Ivri* (pronounced ee-vree), which means Hebrew. The meaning of the name Eber comes from the root *avar* – עבר. Hebrew verbs all come out of a three-letter root. The root of this word *Avar* is spelled *ayin, bet, resh* in Hebrew. As we have said before, this name means to pass through or cross over, and we know Abraham was called a Hebrew because he passed through and crossed over. In Genesis 14:13, he is called a Hebrew for the first time. Hebrew is the English word, but in Hebrew it is *Ivri* – עברי. So let us look at Abraham to see where he crossed over and passed through.

In Genesis 12:5-6 it says, "Abraham took Sarah his wife… Abraham crossed over and passed through the land to Shechem." The basic

---

[1] Tenakh is what is commonly known as the Old Testament, but should be referred to as the Hebrew Scriptures

message is that when Abraham crossed over from his family to God, he passed from the sins of his fathers to the blessings of his heavenly Father. Abraham crossed over to God and received His blessings. עבר *(avar)* is a root word for cross over or pass through. In Genesis 14:13 Abraham was called *Ivri,* a word related to *avar,* which means a Hebrew person, one who has crossed over.

Jacob was a descendent of Abraham; he was a Hebrew, too. In Genesis 32:10 Jacob says, "I have crossed over this Jordan with my staff, and now I have become two companies." Jacob also crossed over. After Jacob crossed over through the test of wrestling with God (v. 24), it says the sun rose on him (v. 31) just as he crossed over the place he named *Penniel,* which means Face of God. It is as if God had the sun rise on him representing the light, the presence and the hope of God, rising upon him. That night he had been in despair, but now he had crossed over from darkness to light.

Another cross-over is found in Deuteronomy 29:12, 13. This is when Moses was unveiling the covenant before the children of Israel. The New King James Bible (NKJV) says, "That you may enter into covenant with the Lord your God, into His oath which the Lord your God makes with you today." But the word enter is really *avar,* cross over. So it should read, "...that you may cross over into the covenant." The word "enter" is weaker, you can enter or exit. But when you cross over, you have literally gone from one place to another physically and spiritually in every way.

In Micah 2:13 it says, "The Breaker will come and lead the sheep out of the fold." The Hebrew text says that the sheep will cross over *(avar)* through the gate. This is a prophecy of Messiah who will lead the children of Israel out of bondage of sin into freedom. The *Brit Hadashah* (New Covenant) says when we come to Yeshua we come from darkness to light. Galatians says that if we are in Messiah, we are of Abraham's seed (Galatians 3:29). It means you crossed over regardless of whether you are Jewish or one from the nations (goyim). When you cross over to God, whether you are aware of it or not, you become a Hebrew by means of engrafting – as someone of Abraham's seed.

Chapter

2

Hebrew Thinking vs. Greek Thinking

There is an awakening going on today to the fact that much of our Biblical interpretations have been dominated by Greek intellectual and philosophical thinking. First God restored the language of Hebrew when He restored the Jewish people to their land. Now there is a move of God to restore Hebraic thinking to those who read the Bible in translation.

The Book of Zachariah describes a conflict between the sons of Zion and the sons of Greece where it says, "I bent Judah as My bow... and raised up your sons, O Zion, against your sons, O Greece..." (Zachariah 9:13). In Hebrew it says, "I will awaken ועוררתי *(ve-o-rahr-ti)* your sons, O Zion, about (against) Greece's sons." The difference in Hebrew is that it will be an awakening, which has begun to happen today.

Let us define what Zion means and what Greece means. Greece in Hebrew is יון *(Yavan)* and comes from the same root as יין *(ya'in)*, meaning wine. *Wine* represents beauty, richness, and fullness. The word Zion, in Hebrew ציון (*Tzion*), on the other hand, and means a desert, a dry and barren land.

If we deal with the difference between Greek and Hebraic thinking, Greek thinking emphasizes the wealth of our ability and our self-confidence, based on who we think we are, whereas in Hebraic thinking, we cannot trust ourselves because we are totally dependent upon God and know there is nothing in ourselves alone worth trusting in. Zion, being the desert, is totally reliant upon revelation from outside itself, meaning revelation from God. Zion is totally empty of anything valuable within itself apart from God. Greek thinking, on the other hand, is dependent upon itself and upon the fullness of human intellect. In the prophesy of Isaiah 53:2 Yeshua is called a shoot out of dry ground who had no form and nothing that would be attractive to us. Scripture says He came as an empty vessel. He even said, "The Son can do nothing of Himself unless it is something He sees the Father doing; for whatever the Father does, these things the Son also does in like manner" (John 5:19). So Yeshua was a Hebrew who best demonstrated Hebraic thinking by being one hundred percent totally dependent upon His Father.

Today in the Western world, we very much trust in our own logic and intellect, even when we are interpreting the word of God. A strong foundation for the power of human intellect was laid when Greek philosophy began to be incorporated into Biblical interpretation. It is interesting that when the Lord created our brains, He created them with two hemispheres, the left and right hemispheres. The left hemisphere deals with information, logic and intellectual thinking. The right hemisphere deals with emotions, pictures and images.

This leads us to explore some of the biblical understanding of the human heart. When we talk about the concept of heart in the Bible, it is not talking about the organ of the heart necessarily.

Rather, it refers to the inner man, the one that lives inside the body. The first time the heart is mentioned is in Genesis 6:5. It says, "Then the Lord saw that the wickedness of man was great on the earth, and that every intent (or imagination) of the thoughts of his heart was only evil continually." Thoughts are largely images. We generally picture what we intend to do. That means that the language of the heart is made up of, or created from, our imagination. The root of the word to imagine is יצר (yatzar), which means to form or to create. "God created man in His own image" (Genesis 1:27). He must have pictured (imagined) Adam before He created him. Here, in Genesis 6:5, the Hebrew word יצר (yetzer) is used for image. We too can imagine because we are made in God's image. Actually in this passage the word yetzer can be interpreted as desire, intent, or imagination. In modern Hebrew the word yatzira means a work of art.

Behind every word in Hebrew is a picture. It is a pictorial language. Even the alphabet was originally pictures. The letter ayin, for instance, is a picture of an eye, the letter mem is a picture of water, and so on. The fact is that when we say a word in our hearts, or imaginations, we see a picture behind the word. This is why two people may hear the same word and interpret it very differently depending on the picture they each imagine. A lot of times disagreements cannot be resolved until the hearts of the opposing parties are healed because the issue is really a heart issue, not an understanding issue. Therefore, the heart is much more important than the intellect.

I believe that God speaks directly to the heart. Psalm 16:8-9 says, "I have set the Lord always before me. Because He is at my right hand I shall not be moved. Therefore my heart is glad and my glory rejoices; my flesh also will rest in hope." Let us go through the meaning of a few words. "I have set" in Hebrew is שויתי (shiviti). This is very difficult to translate in any other language. It comes from the meaning to compare or to make equal. It is a picture that the Psalmist used to describe the right connection between himself and the Lord. It actually says "because He is on my right." It does not say "right hand" in Hebrew. It is important for us to understand what it means for the Lord to be on my right. Scripture describes our connection to Him to be on the right. It has to do with how we perceive Him.

In the Book of Ecclesiastes 10:2 it says, "A wise man's heart is at his right hand, but a fool's heart at his left." The part of our being that understands images is the right hemisphere of our brain. That means that usually we cannot perceive the Lord through our intellect. It must be a matter of the heart. Today we are dominated by left-brain intellectual thinking. Even in our schools, left-brain subjects are required and the right brain electives such as, art and music are the first to be eliminated because of budget limitations – and budgets are matters of left-brain thinking.

The Lord gave us intellect to serve the heart and not the other way around. Intellect is from God, but it is not to dominate our way of perceiving. We can see an application of this in the picture that Ezekiel recounts in Chapter 1, when he saw four living creatures with four faces in the whirlwind. Among the four faces were faces of an ox on the left and a lion on the right. A lion is to be a ruler while an ox is a servant. Today the ox rules from the left and the lion is in a cage, not ruling. This is a very important to understand. The Greek mindset is like an ox (on the left) and not a lion (on the right). So the Greek mindset should not be ruling the issues of the heart. The Hebraic understanding is that we are not to be dominated by intellect, but by listening to God's heart.

The word of God is given to us by the Spirit of God, and it is the same Holy Spirit who is given to us to understand God's word. It is not our intellect that we are to rely upon to understand the word of God. If we could understand with our intellect, why would we need the Holy Spirit? It is revelation by the Spirit that gives us understanding. The intellect is given to us to put the understanding into usable form.[2]

It so happens that the word for understanding – בינה *(binah)* has the same root word as the word for son – בן *(ben)*. As we mentioned before, the Son said that He is totally dependent upon the Father. He only says what He hears the Father saying. The goal of my own life is to develop my ability to hear the voice of God more than reading other people's opinions about the Bible. I do read books, but very selectively. My intent is to encourage you to find your way to connect to God directly and not just fill you with more information.

Many years ago I was at a meeting of a well-known international Bible teacher in Tel Aviv. The miraculous power of God was present in the meetings, and I was impacted by the depth of the teachings of this man. After the meeting, I wanted to buy every teaching recording and every book he wrote. That night I had a dream in which this teacher appeared and was smiling at me. Then his nose changed into a pig's nose and then horns grew up on his head. I woke up with a question, "What is the meaning of this?" The Father spoke to me and gave me the interpretation saying, "This dream is not about this teacher but it is about you. You are about to fall into a trap of following a man rather than following me." After that God instructed me for one year to read no books or listen to recordings of anyone. It was important for me to first learn to receive understanding from Him, and then I could look to other people's interpretations of Scripture.

When we approach the Scriptures with our intellect, we are trying to figure it out on our own. As a result, we have so many competing doctrines. When we begin to apply our minds without our hearts first connecting to God, we have many different pictures in our minds. One of the examples of Greek thinking is compartmentalization. Why is it

---

[2] You can learn more about functionality of the biblical heart at this website: http://www.rediscoveryoftheheart.com. Larry Neppler spent many years learning about the meanings of the heart in the Bible.

that the musical part of many church services is defined by two words; praise describing fast songs and worship defining slow songs? When the Scriptures give examples of worship and sacrifice in Exodus and Leviticus, it does not mention one word about music. We can worship God with or without music. When Abraham took Isaac to sacrifice him – that was the first mention of the word worship (Genesis 22:5). I do not read in this passage that they brought to Mount Moriah, guitars and keyboards along with wood, ropes and a knife.

There are at least two different Hebrew words that are translated into the English word for worship. One is להשתחוות *(le-heesh-tah-ha-vot)* and that means to fall down with your face to the ground before someone, whether it is God or man. In the passage with Abraham offering Isaac the word *leheeshtahavot* is used. It is used often in connection with sacrifices. Also in 1 Samuel 1:3 it says that a man every year went to Shiloh to worship and sacrifice to the Lord. Interesting that the word to sacrifice – in Hebrew להקריב *(le-ha-kriv)* – also means to come close. The purpose here is closeness with God. A great example of this worship is also in Exodus 32, after Israel worshipped the gold calf and Moses pleaded with the Lord not to destroy the nation. After that, Moses set up the Tent of Meeting where he would meet with God outside the camp. There is a description of the Israelites standing at the doors of their tents witnessing the cloud coming down on the Tent of Meeting. As they saw the cloud they would fall down on their faces. This worship was a response to the presence of God. If there is no presence, we are unlikely to enter into that kind of true worship. The second word is לעבוד *(la-a-vod)*, which means to serve or to work as when we serve God. Verse 4 of Exodus 20 commands Israel not to bow down nor serve idols. As a personal note on compartmentalization, I do not care to be labeled Charismatic, Messianic or by any other non-scriptural terms. All that matters to me is the one identity which Yeshua restored for me – that of being a son to God. God calls me by my name and that is good enough for me.

Chapter

3

The Power of
One Letter

We are looking at Hebrew in several different ways. We are looking at it pictorially, as well as unveiling things that have been lost in the translations of different passages of the Hebrew Scriptures. Let us now talk about Hebrew letters. In English one letter generally does not mean anything unless it is put together with at least another letter to form a word. The letters have no meaning in themselves. But in Hebrew each letter has a message and a meaning. One Hebrew letter can speak in at least three different ways – through a picture, through a sound and as numbers. The Hebrew word for letter is *ot* (אות – pronounced as *oht*). It means a sign or a supernatural sign, like the signs that Moses performed before Pharaoh.

There are altogether twenty-two letters, which are all signs in the Hebrew alphabet. There are those in the Rabbinic Community who believe that when God spoke the world into existence, He spoke in Hebrew using words made out of these supernatural letters to form the reality of creation.

The original letters of ancient Hebrew, also called Paleo-Hebrew, are all pictures and even present-day Hebrew is pictorial as well. I call the treasures that we find in the Hebrew Scriptures "nuggets of gold". With this in mind, let us look at one of these Hebrew nuggets. Keep in mind that Hebrew reads right to left, not as English, which reads left to right. Here is the word יהוה which is the holy name of God. Religious Jews do not pronounce this name. Others pronounce it in several different ways. In this book, we will pronounce it by just naming the letters — *yod hey vav hey*. There are four letters in this word, or actually three different letters as one letter appears twice.

Let us look at the pictures that each of those letters convey. The first letter is י (*yod*). It is the smallest letter of the Hebrew alphabet. *Yod* means hand. It is both a picture of a hand as well as the name of the letter. The next letter that appears twice within the name is ה (*hey*). *Hey* means "behold" or "here it is," and represents breath or spirit. The picture is of an open window. And the letter ו (*vav*) means hook, peg or nail. If we know the meanings of these three letters and we look into the word יהוה – *YHWH,* we see a hand, we see behold twice and we see a nail. There almost seems to be a message, does not there? Behold the hand, behold the nail.

Looking more closely, the letter ה (*hey)* appears in the name of God twice. *Hey* makes a sound of breath coming out from our lungs, or like a wind. Like a *hhh* sound. Also, the picture of the word *hey* is like an open window that allows wind to come in or out. The word for breath or wind in Hebrew is *ruach* – רוח (roo-akh), which is also the word for spirit. One of the major representations of the letter *hey* is spirit. According to the Scriptures, what is the chief function of the Spirit of God? I am only going to address the one function that I believe is the major one and that is to pour God's love into our hearts. Romans 5:5 says, "Now hope does not disappoint because the love of God has been poured out in our hearts by the Holy Spirit who was given to us."

We will now see how the letter *hey* is used in other Hebrew words in a meaningful way. The Hebrew word for father is אב (*ahv*). This is made up of the first two letters in the Hebrew alphabet. It is interesting that the first two letters of the Hebrew alphabet form the word *father*. The first letter א *(aleph)* means strength. The next letter, ב *(bet)*, means house. If we just look pictorially at the word father אב – we can see a message there: Strength of the house. Father is the strength of the house, strength of the household. Is it possible that the world is falling apart today because the strength of the house is too often missing? Incidentally, these first two letters, *aleph* and *bet* are where we derive the English word alphabet *(alpha-bet)* from.

If we insert the letter ה *(hey)* into the middle of the word אב – father, a root verb is formed which is a most important word – אהב *(ah-hahv)*, which is a root for the one of the Hebrew words, which means to love. A noun is formed by adding another ה *(hey)* at the end of the word, so that it reads as אהבה *(ahavah)*, meaning love. So all together we have:

God's name		יהוה
Hey		ה
Father	*Av*	אב
To love (root)	*ahav*	אהב
Love (noun)	*ahavah*	אהבה

Even the Hebrew letters clearly indicate that God the Father is the source of love. Love is in the middle (heart) of Him, and what is in the middle (heart) of Him comes out, as the *hey* at the end of the word אהבה *(ahavah)* points out. That means that everything that the Father does, even what we do not understand, has to come from His love. When we look back to the word יהוה again, the name of God, we find that both uses of the letter *hey* are in the same position as in the word *ahavah*. It is an overwhelming picture to me that God is love. This is but one of the examples of the supernatural aspect of the Hebrew language which obviously appears to come from God Himself.

Continuing with the letter ה (*hey*), the Hebrew word אל (*El*) means God, which is made up of the two letters, א (*aleph*) and ל (*lamed*). אל (*El*) is short for the longer word אלוהים (*Elohim*). Again if we look at the letters, א (*aleph*) is strength and ל (*lamed*) means a staff or a rod, which represents power and authority. God or אל is ultimate strength, power and authority. When we put the ה in the middle of אל, another word is created which is the word אהל (*ohel*), which means tent.

| God | *El* | אל |
| Tent | *Ohel* | אהל |

From this we learn that the Being of ultimate strength, power and authority desires a dwelling place with His children where He can pour out His love. He is not interested in living in a tent by Himself but with His children. He is very relational in His nature. He never told Abraham: "In you all the churches will be blessed," but that through him all the families would be blessed. That is why He is the Father and not just the Master of the world.

Now we will look to understand what happened with Abram and Sarai, the original names of Abraham and Sarah. In Hebrew Abram's name is אברם – pronounced Avram. Avram was his original name and it consists of two parts: אב (*Av*) is father and רם (*rahm*) is high or exalted, so his name meant exalted father. God promised him that he would become a great nation (Genesis 12:2). For a great number of years Abram had a problem with this message from the Lord because he and Sarai were childless. In Genesis 17:5 God makes a slight change to his name simply by inserting the letter ה (*hey*) from His own name. He was אברם (Avram), now he becomes אברהם (Avraham). His name now reflects that he received the heavenly breath or Spirit of God into his being/nature and began to represent His Heavenly Father's love. Eventually he will be able to fulfill his calling to be a father to many nations. And what does that mean? He now becomes a representative of Father's love to all the families of the earth (Isaiah 51:2).

Now let us see what happens to Sarah. Her name originally was שרי (Sarai, pronounced Sara-ee), which means my princess. When the Lord changed Sarai's name, the י (*yod*) was replaced with ה (*hey*). Now her name also indicates that she received the breath or Spirit of the Father. I believe this addition of ה is a prophetic picture of being born of the Spirit. When we are born from above the Spirit enters into us and seals us, the seal that indicate that we belong to God (Ephesians 1:13). In that sense, we all receive the letter ה from God's name and as the Spirit enters into us, His love fills our hearts. With this in mind, let us look at another Hebrew nugget.

Chapter

4   Hebrew and God

Hebrew is always God-focused! The first letter, א (*aleph*) is a letter that represents God Himself for several reasons. The very first word that begins with א in the Scriptures is אלוהים (*Elohim*). The word אלף (*aleph*) relates to the word אלוף (*aluf*, pronounced ah-loof), which means The Most Powerful. No one can overpower God. In Modern Hebrew it also means champion. *Aleph* is a composite letter, which consists of a slanted ו *vav* in the middle and two יי *yods*, one at the top right and one at the bottom left to create the letter.

In the Hebrew language every letter is also a number: *Alef* is one, *bet* is two, *gimmel* is three and so on. The number of the composite *aleph*, that is the sum total of the numerical parts that make up *aleph*, is twenty-six: *Yod* is 10 twice, and *vav* is 6 = 26. So what is the significance? 26 is the numerical value of God's name, יהוה (YHWH). Let us look at the Hebrew word for man. In the Bible there are three out of four words for man that begin with א *(alef)*: אדם (*Adam*, pronounced Adahm), אנוש (*e-nowsh* pronounced ee-know-sh) and איש (*eesh*). Man is made in God's image and *alef* indicates his connection with God. When we look at the word אדם (*Adam*) it has an א (*aleph*) and the rest of it spells דם (*dam*, pronounced dahm) which is the word for blood. So the word Adam has God and man in it. *Aleph* – our connection with יהוה – is what separates us from animals, who also have blood, "for the life of the flesh is in the blood" (Leviticus 17:11). But if we do not have God in our lives, we are slaves to the desires of the flesh, which are in the blood.

The other way to look at the word *Adam* is to look at each letter that makes up the Hebrew word אדם separately: א (*aleph*) represents God, ד (*dalet*) represent a door and מ (*mem*) represents water. The message of the word *Adam* is God's door into the water. Life comes from water. A baby is formed in the water of the womb. Remember that Yeshua said to Nicodemus, "Unless one is born of water and the Spirit, you cannot enter the Kingdom of God" (John 3:5). Being born of water is not enough though; we need the Spirit to be born of God.

We can see many things in this. We could say that man is God's door into life, which Yeshua fulfilled because He said, "I am the door" (John 10:7, 9). There are many things that can be seen in this picture other than what I have just shown you. Use your imagination and let God show you more.

Now let us look at the word איש (*ish*). It is spelled *aleph, yod, shin*. Man is איש (*ish*), and woman is אשה (*ishah* pronounced ee-shah). They each have two letters that are common to them, א (*aleph*) and ש (*shin*). And each has a letter that is unique to them. Man has a י (*yod*) and the woman has a ה (*hey*). Both י (*yod*) and ה (*hey*) relate to the name of God, יהוה (*YHWH*). There are a few times in Scripture, when the name of God is written as an acronym, like this יה, using the first and last letter. The word הללויה (*hallelu-yah*) is two words: הללו (*hallelu*), which is praise, and יה (*yah*), which is an acronym for יהוה.

י (*Yod*) is a picture of man's connection to God. י (*Yod*) represents hand or action. Women relate to God more easily by the spirit. This relationship is represented by ה (hey) representing Spirit. My opinion is that it is not difficult to see the sensitivity to the spirit more in women than in men. This sensitivity to the spirit is the very help that man needs especially after he fell, but we will talk more about that later. It is interesting that we can only find the fullness of God in both the words for man and woman, but each one by themselves carries only part. A man and woman together complete the presence of the fullness of God.

So looking at the collective words for man and woman, if the presence of God is missing in a man and woman's relationship, that is, י (yod) and ה (hey) are no longer present, then we have the letters א (aleph) and ש (shin) left, forming the word אש (esh), which is fire. When God is not there, the relationship can be one of fire, which can be destructive. When we take out the *yod* and the *hey*, which represent God, both the word for man and woman are left with the same fire, which breaks down and burns up the bridge God meant to connect man and woman together – and that bridge is Him. Without this understanding, they no longer see their uniqueness in God. They come into competition with one another rather than live in harmony with one another. All this insight comes from just looking at the Hebrew letters. No other language that I am aware of indicates all of this, and provides examples of how we can see God Himself in all parts of the language.

Chapter

5   Insight into Torah

There are two reasons why I do not like the name "Old Testament." The first reason is that it is not old. The second reason is it is not a testament. A testament is basically a document having to do with someone's death. And a testament is not a covenant. The Jewish people refer to the whole of the Hebrew Scriptures as the *Tenakh*. This is how it is written in Hebrew: תנ״ך. *Tenakh* consists of three parts: תורה (*Torah*), which are the teachings, נביאים (*Naviim*) which are the prophets, and כתובים (*Ketuvim*) which are the writings. We see it is the first letter of each of these sections of the Bible, T-N-K that make up the acronym for *Tenakh*. The word *Torah* comes from the root ירה (*yarah*) which means to shoot at a target. It is interesting that the word חטא (*chata*), which is the Hebrew word for sin, means to miss the target.

Torah consists of the first five books of the *Tenakh*. Jewish tradition puts them together as *Torah*, and attributes them to the writings of Moses. Let us talk about the names of the five books. In English the first is called Genesis, in Hebrew בראשית (*Beresheet*), which means "in the beginning". Truly, that book is about beginnings. It talks about the beginning of the creation of the world, the beginning of mankind, the beginning of the nations of the world, and the beginning of the nation of Israel – it is all in there.

The next book is called Exodus in the English Bible. The story of Israel's exodus from Egypt covers only part of the book and the rest of the book deals with other topics. In Hebrew that book is called שמות (Shemot), which means "names". This is a book about the people whose names are in God's book.

The next book is called Leviticus in English, probably because it deals with the tribe of Levi who were the priests. Many people think today that the Levites were done away with so why bother reading it. But there is much revelation in there about living holy lives and after all, we who are believers are now to be as priests. In Hebrew, the book of Leviticus is called ויקרא (Vayekra) and it means "and He called". This book is about those who are called by God. If the second book is about belonging, the third book is about calling.

The fourth book is called Numbers in English, probably because it largely deals with the numbering of the different tribes of Israel. But in Hebrew it is called במדבר (Bamidbar), which means "in the wilderness". It is really about the journey of God's people through the wilderness. The root word for wilderness is דבר (davar), which also means "word". It looks like God took His people into the wilderness so they would learn to hear His voice. There is a scripture in Isaiah 40 which says, "קוֹל קוֹרֵא בַּמִּדְבָּר" - "The voice cries out in the wilderness."

The last book of *Torah* is called Deuteronomy in English, which means "second law." Many people erroneously say, "We do not have to keep the first law so why bother about the second one", but these are God's words. In Hebrew it is called דברים (Devarim), which means "words," plural. It comes from the first sentence: "These are the words which Moses spoke to all Israel". So this book is a continuation of God's words, and God's voice.

In Genesis chapter one, we are going to look at the very first word from several angles. This word is translated: "In the beginning" and it looks like this:

בראשית

There are many messages packed into the first word in the Bible. The word בראשית, pronounced *beh-reh-sheet*, translates as "in the beginning." It has three parts: ב means "in," ראש (resh or rosh) is "head" and ית (eet) is "of."

ב-ראש-ית

beh – resh – eet.

ב (*bet*) is the prefix represented by second letter of Hebrew alphabet. The meaning of the letter *bet* is the house. The first letter gives an indication that there is an idea of a house here. The middle part is ראש (*rosh*) – head, and it is the main concept here. It points to the fact that there is somebody here at the head of things, who is the first and who is in charge. What does the head do? It thinks. If the first part means the house, could it be that somebody who is in charge had a thought to build a house? We can find the support for it if we take the first three letters of the word Beresheet they become ברא (*barah*). Barah means to create. God wanted to create, He wanted to build a house and make a family for Himself. This word ברא (*barah*) is inside the first word of the sentence בראשית (beresheet), as well as it is the second word of the sentence. בראשית ברא *(beresheet barah)*, indicates that the thought is about creating.

The last part: ית (*eet*) would be understood as "of." For example: in the beginning <u>of</u> things, at the head <u>of</u> creation. What does it mean, "to begin"? In order to build a house, you have to have a plan, you have to think. This is why everything starts in the head – ראש *(rosh)*. Everything started with a thought. When a thought is carried by sound waves, it is called a word. John in chapter one begins by saying, "In the beginning was the word and the word was with God."

The third section of the word בראשית – (beresheet) consists of two letters: י (yod) and ת (tav). י (yod), as we have seen, means hand. Hand indicates action. God began to take action, to act on His thought, on His idea. The last letter is ת (tav), which means a supernatural sign. God moved on His thought supernaturally.

Now, if we take the first two letters of the word בראשית (beresheet) – בר, they form the word son. So the first word that can be formed is son! Bar is son. Isn't that amazing? The Son was in the beginning with God.

There are two Hebrew words for son, one is בן (ben) which has several meanings, such as builder and knowledge. In Proverbs it mentions a lot about wisdom and knowledge as בינה (bina). The other word for son is בר (bar), which is what we read in Beresheet. It is also mentioned in Psalm 2 where it says, "Kiss the son lest He be angry." That is the word bar for son. Another meaning of the word bar is grain and it is also inside the word ברור (barur) – pure. Yeshua said, speaking of Himself and His death, "Unless the grain falls and dies it will not produce life." We also know that Yeshua is the "bread of life" and He is pure.

If we see the first two letters of Beresheet forming the word בר (bar), son, the rest of it is אשית (asheet). This word is a future form of the word, which means "to place". It is used in Psalm 110:1 in exactly the same form, which says in a translation of the Hebrew, "YHWH said to my Lord, 'Sit at my right hand till I place your enemies as your footstool.'" There is the hint here, in the first word of the Bible, beresheet, when we link it with the Psalm 110, which says that the son will have enemies placed under His feet.

We have gone very superficially into the first word of the first book of the Bible. There is a lot more to explore. Tell me if this does not make you think there is something very supernatural about this language? Books could be written and messages taught on this one word alone.

Chapter
6

"I will be..."

"אהיה" —

בראשית ברא אלהים את השמים ואת הארץ

The first sentence in the Hebrew Bible consists exactly of seven words. We can place those seven words on a *menorah*, a lampstand. A short Hebrew word in the middle of the sentence falls on the trunk of the *menorah*, a lampstand, which represents a tree with branches. It is a tree of life. This little word in the middle that is a unique part of Hebrew grammar is את *(et)*. It consists of the first letter of the Hebrew alphabet and the last, *aleph* and *tav*, with the message of these letters being the first and the last. I cannot help but see Yeshua here as being the trunk of the tree who said to His disciples, "I am the vine, you are the branches", and who also said, "I am the beginning and the end", which the *aleph* and the *tav* represent.

In Exodus 3:13-14, Moses asked God, "…and if they say to me, 'What is His name?' What shall I tell them?" And God said to Moses, "I am Who I am. Thus you shall say to the children of Israel, 'I am has sent me to you.'" Where it says, "I am Who I am" in Hebrew it says, "אהיה אשר אהיה" – *"Eheyeh asher eheyeh"*, which literally means "I will be who I will be". At the basis of God's name is the Hebrew word היה *(hayah),* which means "to be". Most times His name appears as יהוה *(YHWH)*. When the Israelites asked Moses what is the name of this God – in those days the understanding of this question would be that God's name would reflect His actions. So when they asked His name, they were really asking, "What is He going to do?"

Why, in this case, would God's name be in the future tense as in I will be, or אהיה *(eheyeh)*? In just one verse before, in verse 12, God was speaking to Moses and He said, "**I will** certainly **be** with you – אהיה עמך. And this shall be a sign to you that I have sent you, when you have brought the people out of Egypt, you will serve God on this mountain."

In Exodus 4:11, 12 in response to Moses' statement, "I am a man of slow speech", God said to him, "Who has made man's mouth or who makes the mute, the deaf, the seeing or the blind? Have not I the Lord? Now therefore, go, and I will be with your mouth and teach you what you shall say." In both the verses we just read, when God says, "I will be" in Hebrew, He is saying, *eheyeh*. So when Moses asked about God's name, that is what God is saying, "I will be", meaning "I will be with you. I will go before you", even, "I will be with your mouth", In a sense what I see here is God saying, "You cannot even imagine what I can do for you and through you."

Perhaps, we can even look at it from a different angle. When God said to Moses, "I will be who I will be", in a sense He is trying to say do not try to figure Me out. It is Greek thinking that tries to figure out God. But who can figure out God who lives outside of time and space? So He is saying, "You cannot figure Me out, just know that I will go before you!"

Chapter

7   More from Genesis

Let us go back to Genesis, chapter one, verse 2. "And the earth was without form and void and darkness was on the face of the deep and the Spirit of God was hovering over the face of the waters." Let us look at the word for hovering, which is מרחפת *(merakhefet)*. The root is רחף *(rakhaf)*. This verb is in the feminine gender indicating that the Spirit of God in *Tenakh* is always represented in the feminine gender. If it were in the masculine gender the verb would be *merakhef,* without the *'et'* ending which is what makes it feminine.

When we look at the root of the meaning of *rakhaf,* it means to hover, to fly, shake, tremble, brood, glide, float and vibrate. This is possibly the beginning of sound and light frequencies. Scientists are discovering today that at the basis of all matter are sound and light frequencies. So when God spoke the world into existence, He used the sound of His voice and when the Spirit of God touched the inert matter, it began to vibrate.

Because the Holy Spirit is described grammatically in the feminine gender and one of the meanings of the word *merakhefet* is to brood, we can see a picture of a mother bird brooding over her young. It is almost like the Spirit of God brings nurturance to that which has no life in order to bring life to it. There is a reflection on how in the book of Matthew, Yeshua is speaking to Jerusalem and He says, "Jerusalem, Jerusalem, ... how often I have wanted to gather your children together as a mother hen gathers her chicks" (23:37). He is painting a picture of having an impulse of a mother bird to nurture her young.

There are several passages where God acts in the feminine. We will not cover them all but here's a special one. Where Zion says, "The Lord has forsaken me" and God responds with saying, "Can a woman forget her nursing child....but I will not forget you" (Isaiah 49:15). We mentioned earlier that the letter *hey* that represents God's Spirit is present in the word אשה *(ishah)* meaning woman. Would it be possible, because women are so sensitive to the spirit of God, that one of the reasons that Adam needed a woman is to help with things of the Spirit? There is no doubt that women are much quicker to notice sin than men. For example, when the two are watching the same movie women may be more sensitive to something unclean in the movie. For that matter, what is more common: intercessory prayer meetings led by men or women?

Let us now look at 1 Peter 3:7. "Husbands, likewise, dwell with them with understanding, giving honor to the wife, as to the weaker vessel, and as being heirs together of the grace of life, that your prayers may not be hindered." In this passage, it says if the husbands do not understand their wives, then their prayers may be hindered. What is the reasoning behind this? Most men will admit it is not so easy to understand women. That is why someone even wrote a book called, "Men are from Mars, Women are from Venus". In this passage in 1 Peter husbands are commanded to understand their wives. Why?

Yeshua spoke of the Spirit of God, who would come and tell us what the Father wants us to know. The Father speaks and it is the Spirit that brings the words of the Father to us. We have just learned that the Spirit of God operates in the feminine, so if the husbands do not understand their wives, they are less likely to understand the Spirit. In which case, their prayers may be more motivated by their intellect, than by the Spirit. Even if they do not have a wife, they still have women in their lives they have to learn to understand. Since God generally answers prayers that are initiated by the Spirit in the first place, if the prayers are not in agreement with the Spirit of God, those prayers could be hindered from being answered.

I am certainly not saying everything women say is correct, and men are always wrong. All I am saying is that, if a man learns to correctly interpret what a woman is saying, it will be easier for him to interpret what God is saying. In this, women are great helpers to men.

I would like to add something here while on the subject of women, and that is the reason for the assault against the feminine – which was initiated by the forces of darkness. Let us see exactly what happened with Adam and Eve in the Garden. When the enemy offered the woman a fruit from the forbidden tree, where was the man at that moment? It appears he was right next to her, listening to the whole conversation. She gave the fruit to "her husband (who was) with her" (Gen.3:6), so he was right there. The commandment was given to him and not to her. He did absolutely nothing to prevent the spirit of darkness from speaking to his wife. After they fell into sin, God confronted them both and this is how Adam answered: "The woman who You gave to me to be with me, she gave me of the fruit of the tree and I ate" (Gen.3:12). Rather than simply admitting his fault and repenting, he shifted the blame to her and it even looks like he was blaming God Himself for giving him the woman.

Many men today inherited this problem from Adam of being too defensive, not really wanting to admit to their own fault. How did the woman answer? "The serpent deceived me and I ate" (Gen.3:13). She simply said what happened. Later on when the Scripture relates this story in the *Brit Hadashah* (New Testament) it says Adam sinned but the woman was deceived. It does not look like there was any blame shifting in the woman's response. Maybe because of this, something interesting happens next.

God is speaking to the serpent. He says, "I will put enmity between you and the woman, and between your seed and her seed." (Gen.3:15). We can look at this statement from several different angles. One, there was enmity placed between the serpent and the woman. Enmity means war in which the serpent is the enemy of the woman and the woman is the enemy of the serpent. Not many people see her, or women, as the serpent's enemy. Maybe it is because of this that women are so much stronger in the Spirit. Because she did not shift the blame, God has given her authority over the enemy. She is going to produce a seed that will destroy him. Later we will see how that seed manifests. What we see today in every culture, nation and religion, is that women are attacked. Especially where there is more darkness, there is always more oppression of the women. In Islam a woman is considered to have only half the value of a man. The war against the feminine is a war against God. Women are made in God's image just as men are. It is my opinion that God put some of His best qualities in women.

When God said the man needs a helper, today when we think of the word helper, we think that the man is the main one and he needs someone to run his chores. The word for helper or helpmate, refers to God helping His people rather than someone who is to serve another. We see signs that say, "Hired Help Needed". The meaning of this word has totally changed. It is good to note that inside the Hebrew word helper, עזר *(ezer)*, there is the word עז *(ehz)* which relates to the word עוז *(oz)* which means power. Woman was created to be a powerful helper to man. A separate book could be written about what men could learn about God by listening to women. It is time to put our pride down, men, and humble ourselves. God made us heads but a head without a heart will not survive.

Chapter

8

Holiness and Separation

What is holiness? It comes from the Hebrew word קדוש (*kadosh*). It has several different meanings. It is a verb that means to set apart as in to separate or to dedicate. And in a pictorial sense everything that God fills with His presence is holy. Like in the place of the burning bush, God quickly let Moses know that the ground on which he stood was holy (Exodus 3:5) and set apart from the ground around that area. God even accomplished creation through the process of separating. First He separated light from darkness, then He separated waters from waters, so there were waters above and waters below. He divided them with an expanse (firmament). The waters under the expanse were separated into the dry land and the seas.

The trees were separated, each one according to its seed, and eventually God separated the seventh day from the other six days. In that day He divided rest from work. When God gave the Torah to Moses He included many aspects that deal with separation or the division of good from evil, clean from unclean, honest from dishonest, and so forth.

For instance, in Leviticus (*Vayeekra*), Chapter 11, the food of the children of Israel was separated from what they were not permitted to eat. Here we have qualifications for the animals they were allowed to eat. They must have split hooves and chew the cud. What do split hooves represent on the legs? It is a picture of a walk separated unto God. One animal that has a split hoof but does not chew cud is a pig. It may be a picture of someone who says I have a separate walk unto God but eats whatever he wants, with no discernment about what goes into him. A person like that could be likened to a pig. There are people that call themselves believers, who do not have any spiritual sensitivity as to what they put into themselves, naturally and spiritually.

To give you a better meaning of some other qualifications of a clean animal, let us look at what it means to chew the cud. When we look at the Hebrew text, the actual words, מעלת גרה (ma'alat gerah) literally mean lifting up, so this refers to lifting up the cud. The reason it is translated as chewing the cud is that clean animals regurgitate, which means they bring up the food from their stomachs to be chewed again. Before we talk about the meaning of the words lifting up, I want to talk about the qualification of the edible insect. It seems repulsive by Western culture, but there was a kind of grasshopper that was allowed to be eaten. We find that in Leviticus 11:21. There it says the grasshoppers, which can be eaten have jointed legs above their feet. The word above is ממעל (mi-me'al) has the same root as the word ma'alat gerah for lifted up or above.

At the end of Chapter 11, after we finish reading about the qualifications of the different animals that can or cannot be eaten, in verse 44 we read: "For I am YHWH, your God. Sanctify (or separate) yourselves for I am holy." This verse is quoted in 1 Peter 1:16, "Be holy for I am holy." The next verse says, "For I am YHWH that brought you up, (literally lifted you up, המעלה (hama-aleh) from the land of Egypt." The symbols in this chapter describe the setting apart of God's people, that they have been separated and lifted up into the realm above. This is one of the foundational chapters to best understand what holiness is because of the symbolism. It is more than about healthy food versus non-healthy food. Read it for yourself and see what God shows you.

Symbolism of chewing the cud of the animals considered to be clean are the ones which "value" the food they have and bring it up again and again to glean the most nutrition from it. The clean believer is one who brings back the Words of the Lord into remembrance time and again just as Joshua was told to meditate on God's words day and night (Joshua 1:8). He was, in effect, chewing the cud... not just letting the valuable words of God pass by after one "chewing" like a pig would.

With this in mind, let us go back to Genesis 1:6. God says, "Let there be a firmament in the midst of the waters." He is dividing waters from waters. I want to mention how we see the first chapter symbolically in relationship to God's people. There has to be a reason why God choose to create the world in six days. God is all-powerful. He could have chosen to create everything in one moment. Yet He spread it out to six days plus a day of rest. Could it be that for those who come to the Lord and are born from above and are called "new creations", that there is a lesson for us in the process of how God's image is unveiled in us? For example, when we are born from above, we enter into our own first day of our spiritual creation. What happened on the first day of creation? God said, "Let there be light" and He divided light from darkness.

What happens to us when we become believers in Yeshua? God's light enters into our hearts and the process of dividing light from darkness begins in our lives. Then we are ready to enter the second day of creation, which we are talking about now, when God divided waters from waters. What is water a symbol of? Waters are symbolic of God's word. Isaiah 55:10, 11 says, "For as the rain comes down, and the snow from heaven, and do not return there, but water the earth... so shall My word be that goes forth from My mouth."

Another confirmation of that symbol of water is, "Husbands, love your wives, just as Messiah also loved the *kehilah* (congregation of believers) and gave Himself for her, that He might sanctify and cleanse her with the washing of water by the word" (Ephesians 5:25, 26). So water represents the word of God. We also see the order God wants to bring into our lives when we enter into the "second day" as a new creation, as He begins to put things in godly order in our lives through His word.

Paul spoke to Timothy about "rightly dividing the word of truth" (1 Timothy 2:15). That means, the word can be interpreted from above by the Spirit or it can be carnally interpreted by the mind of the flesh. One day, Yeshua spoke to people who knew the word very well about the reason why they did not understand what He was saying. He said to them, "You are from beneath; I am from above. You are of this world; I am not of this world" (John 8:23). They knew the word but they were unable to "rightly divide" it to find the truth.

Every day represents some progress in our growth in the Lord. This is not the theme of this book, but the ultimate goal here is that man is unveiled in God's image as seen in day six, when man was created. Day seven is about coming into sonship. What I mean by that is that the seventh day is a day of rest when God Himself abstained from His work. Later He asked man to abstain from his work one day a week, so he could develop relationship with the Father. And "the Son can do nothing of Himself, unless *it is* something He sees the Father doing" (John 5:19). Our service to God should flow out from the place of rest!

Let us look back to seeing what God did when He divided the waters with the expanse. In Hebrew this is called רקיע (*rakiah* - rah-kee-ah). It is also translated firmament, but expanse more closely expresses the Hebrew. "God made the expanse which divided the waters." He divided the waters *with* the expanse. The expanse was the separating wall. God calls this expanse "heavens", plural. *Rakia* comes from the verb that means to stomp as with your feet or to spread. It is also a biblical name for sky and heavens. If we would like to follow the development in the modern language, the word *rakiah* also means background. The sky is like a background. What is the meaning of spread? The scientists tell us the universe is constantly expanding or spreading.

If this *rakiah* is called heaven, it means there is a realm above the heavens. In the physical world this represents sky, which in Hebrew has to do with heaven and sky. They are the same word, *shamayim*. *Sham* means there and *mayim* means waters. The real meaning is "waters are there".

In the Scriptures there is a realm called "waters above" which is the realm above the heavens. Psalm 148:4 says, "Praise Him, you heavens of heavens, and you waters above the heavens!" In the physical realm, heavens represent sky. But in the spirit realm there is a parallel to the physical realm, because the physical realm mirrors that which is in the spiritual realm, so these waters have to be there above the heavens. Indeed, in Ezekiel chapter one where the throne of God is set above the firmament (*rakiah*). There is a likeness to man of Him who sits on the throne whom I believe is Yeshua Himself. He is above *rakiah*, and if we are believers, that is the realm where God has placed us when He "raised us up together, and made us sit together in the heavenly places in Messiah Yeshua" (Ephesians 2:6).

I wonder what Paul saw when he went to the third heaven. Is that the realm he experienced? Is the third heaven the realm above *rakiah*? Because if this is where the throne of God is, that is where we belong, with Him. When God created us He placed us underneath the heavens, in the realm below *rakiah*. This realm is an earthly realm. It may have a physical life but it is void of the spiritual realm, so in that essence, it is a realm of spiritual darkness. Man was placed in that realm below *rakiah* to be God's light and also to conquer this darkness. Our bodies are made of earth so our physical bodies belong to the realm underneath. But the life of the Spirit in us is from above. Man is planted like a seed where the seed must die in order to produce new life. In that sense, we are called to die daily to the things of spiritual darkness. Yeshua really manifested this by dying so that the new life could be produced. This is about destiny, but it comes out of creation. In Hebrew we can really see this.

What we are talking about here is creation and holiness and how we are called to live in the realm of spiritual darkness and yet we belong in the realm above. If our life comes from the realm above, then the way we think and interpret the word and everything else should come from above. The true meaning of holiness is that in every part of our beings we belong to Him, though we function in a different realm. Yeshua said, "I am not of this world" (John 8:23). So, what is our main purpose in how we are becoming like Him? It is to transform the environment, to impact the world with heavenly light. Because one day, "...the earth will be filled with the knowledge of the glory of the LORD, as the waters cover the sea" (Habakkuk 2:14).

Chapter

9   On Being Fruitful

Genesis 2:3 says "God blessed the seventh day and sanctified it because in it He rested from all His works which God created and made." There is a small but very significant difference in the way it reads in English from the Hebrew text. In English the phrase "created and made" gives the sense that everything was finished. But in Hebrew the word לעשות *(la-asoht)* is in the infinitive, meaning "to make" or "to do". So a correct translation of the sentence would be, "And God blessed the seventh day and separated it because in it He rested from all His works that He created to do / to make." It gives the sense that something else is to be done. This is how it looks in Hebrew:

וַיְבָרֶךְ אֱלֹהִים אֶת־יוֹם הַשְּׁבִיעִי וַיְקַדֵּשׁ אֹתוֹ כִּי בוֹ שָׁבַת מִכָּל־מְלַאכְתּוֹ אֲשֶׁר־בָּרָא אֱלֹהִים לַעֲשׂוֹת

Most translations, with rare exception, put it in the past tense as if God finished the creation and there was nothing left to do. But why would it say לעשות *(la-asoht* -"to do") in Hebrew? From what I see now, God finished His part but He left it for man to complete something. Let us find out if there is any place in Scripture where we can see what I just said about completion. Isaiah 45:7 is a very strange verse. It refers to creation. In this verse the Lord is saying, "I form the light and create darkness. I make peace and create calamity. I, the Lord, do all these things." Some translators did not want to translate the Hebrew word רע (*ra*) as evil, so the King James Version translated it as calamity, saying that God creates calamity because it would seem to be blasphemy to think that God would create evil.

But if we look at this verse from a Hebrew perspective, we see a description of two opposites. In the second part, where it refers to peace and evil, peace which in Hebrew is שלום (*shalom*), and רע (*ra*) which translates as evil, mean that according to this picture, רע (*ra*) is the opposite of שלום (*shalom*). So this indicates that whatever is opposite of *shalom* biblically, falls into the realm of רע (*ra*). It is important, then, to know the meaning of the word *shalom*. Most people today know the translation of that word as peace, but the word שלום (*shalom*) relates to the verb שילם (*shilem*) which means to complete. The opposite of peace then would mean incompletion.

Maybe Paul understood this when he said in Romans 8:19, "For the earnest expectation of the creation eagerly waits for the revealing of the sons of God." It seems that God charged us with doing something in relationship to the redemption of the creation which I believe we collectively, as the whole body of Messiah, will not be able to accomplish until we *together* come into the fullness of "sonship". Creation is waiting for the fullness of God's sons to become reality. The Son of God came and prepared a way for us to come into this fullness of sonship.

Now, let us look at the place where God charged mankind with a task after mankind was created. We have seen that God created the universe with something left to complete. What was it? In Genesis 1:28 it says, "And God blessed them (mankind) and he said to them, be fruitful and multiply and replenish the earth and subdue it and have dominion over the fish of the sea, birds of the air and everything that creeps".

The first part, to be fruitful and multiply, is obvious. Moving on, the word subdue is כבש (ka-vahsh) and it means to conquer. They were to conquer the earth. The other word, rule, is רדה (ra-dah). If everything was perfect, what was there to subdue and conquer? Basically God said to go to war. As I said before, because man was placed in the realm of spiritual darkness, man was charged with conquering it. Instead of overcoming the darkness, in Genesis 3, man made an agreement with darkness and became a slave to it. Now he was in need of redemption, which was accomplished by Yeshua, the second Adam, who paid the price of the sin of the first Adam. Now that we have been redeemed, Yeshua has done His part in defeating darkness. We still have to face our part in overcoming darkness.

There is another aspect of the question of completion. God created the universe to do something with it. Man and woman are created in God's image. What does it mean to be made in God's image? One of the answers is that God is creator and he gave us also the ability to create. We are little creators. God is a big creator. God can create life and so can we. But for us it takes male and female whereas God does it all by himself. God created the universe, and we can create technology to help us in life. You see God created material with which we can do something. I think it is the reason why in Genesis chapter 2, verse 3 it really says, "He rested from all His work which He had created to do" and not "created and made" as the English translators interpreted it. We spoke in the previous chapters that our heart is a creative engine. It uses imagination to create ideas, thoughts that eventually can become a reality. If our creativity is submitted to God we become co-builders of His kingdom. And if not, then we create our own kingdoms where, realize it or not, we have given all authority to the prince of darkness. Either way, we ultimately contribute to building one kingdom or the other with what we do.

Chapter 10

Appointments with God

The word מועד (*moed*) is used in Leviticus 23:2 referring to the appointed times of God. There is a weekly appointed time with God called שבת (*Shabbat*) and yearly appointed times that include Passover, Unleavened Bread, Sheaf of First Fruits, Feast of Weeks, and what Scripture calls the memorial blowing of trumpets, and then the Day of Atonement and finally, the Feast of Booths. There are seven of these appointed times, not including *Shabbat*. Shabbat is the weekly מועד (*moed*).

Note that in Genesis, God said, "Let there be lights in the firmament of the heavens to divide the day from the night; and let them be for signs and seasons, and for days and years" (Genesis 1:14). What was being set in order are God's appointments and not four seasons of the year. As was said earlier, the word for sign is אות (*oht*), which also means miracle. Miracles or signs often occurred in the past on God's appointed times. And there is no reason to believe they cannot happen now or in the future during these same appointed times.

These מועדים (*moedim*) are really cycles of God, which He Himself arranged on the fourth day of His creation. The fourth day is when the cycles in general were set in place, when God created the sun, moon and stars. We know that the planets rotate. Everything in the universe is in a pattern of cycles. It would be impossible to measure time in the first three days of creation since there was no sun and moon. We can begin to measure time only from the fourth day of creation.

Since the מועדים *(moedim)* are the cycles of God, this means that God Himself operates in these cycles. Two thousand years ago believers got away from these cycles due to the influence of Constantine and the church fathers.[3] But God never abandoned the cycles. He still operates in them, and if we begin to understand the cycles as His appointed times to be with us, we begin to see that our lives also cycle according to the מועדים *(moedim)*, whether we understand their significance or not.

We live in cycles. Weekly cycles start with the first day and go on till the last day and then we begin again. In the yearly cycle we begin with the first month and go to the last month and start the whole thing over again. It looks like we are not going from Point A to Point B; rather we always come back to the same place of a cycle where we started. If we walk with God, it is like walking around a mountain. When we come back to the same side of the mountain, we are actually higher than we were before because we are always growing in God. The enemy has his own cycles, except when we go on his cycles we are descending, always going lower.

According to the Scriptures, the beginning of the cycles is in spring with Passover because in Exodus God said, "This month shall be your beginning of months; it shall be the first month of the year to you" (12:2). When we come to Passover there is an experience of beginning something new, even if we have failed in the past. We can always begin again, because God provides for us to begin again with a new hope. In the course of our lives we go from Passover to the

---

[3] The **Church Fathers, Early Church Fathers, Christian Fathers**, or **Fathers of the Church** are ancient and generally influential Christian theologians, some of whom were eminent teachers and great bishops.

Feast of Booths, and then we will end up at Passover again to begin once more.

The seven appointed times are divided into three seasons: 1) Passover season, (*Pesach in* Hebrew) which includes Passover, Unleavened Bread, and the Sheaf of the First Fruits; 2) the season of the Feast of Weeks (*Shavuot*); and 3) the season of the Feast of Booths (*Sukkot*) which consists of the Feast of Booths, the day of the Blowing of Trumpets *(Yom HaTeruah),* and the Day of Atonement *(Yom Kippur).* Both the season of Passover and the season of the *Feast of Booths* consist of three feasts, while *Shavuot* has only one stand-alone feast. To get an easier picture of what has been said, we need to look at the chart below:

Pesach (Passover) season:
Includes Passover, Unleavened Bread, and the Sheaf of First Fruits.

Shavuot (the Feast of Weeks) season:
A stand-alone feast. It is also known as Pentecost.

Sukkot (Feast of Booths) season:
Includes Feasts of Booths, Day of Blowing of Trumpets, and the Day of Atonement.

There is a commandment for man to come before the Lord during all three of these seasons, that is three times a year as indicated in Exodus 34:23. In all three seasons there is a harvest. Harvests are all about fruit. When we relate harvest to ourselves, we remember the words of Yeshua who said, "By this My Father is glorified, that you bear much fruit; so you will be My disciples" (John 15:8). So our lives in the Lord are parallel to the harvest. The Scriptures speak of the fruit of the spirit and fruits of the flesh. The Father will always plant the seed of love in our lives expecting it to grow into fruit of the Spirit. The enemy also plants his seeds, which grow and become fruits of the flesh — such as greed, bitterness, unforgiveness and lust.

It is often that God determines a certain time to uproot the cause of the bad fruit or tares from our lives.

Yom Kippur symbolizes the Day of Judgment. It is at this time that I believe the anointing is released for uprooting and deliverance. Not that deliverance cannot be done at other times if God so leads, but it is my conviction that Yom Kippur holds a deliverance anointing, since this day is designed for this particular purpose. This is when the Father is willing to release sufficient power and anointing to deal with our strongholds. In our life, we have come into this holiday with that expectation in the past and have sensed the power of deliverance in both the Day of Atonement and the Day of the Blowing of the Trumpets.

On the Day of Atonement (*Yom Kippur*), metaphorically speaking, all the filth that we have picked up from walking through the desert is washed away. Now we can enter the following Feast of Booths (*Sukkot*) and experience seven days of rejoicing before the Lord unencumbered by sin. This is a time when we have opportunity to come into the fullness of our potential in the Lord and to continue for the next six months when we come to the beginning of a new cycle again.

These feasts are a gift from the Father to all his people, not just the Jewish people. I have noticed that many believers who come to the period after *Sukkot* (which happens to come as the Christmas season approaches) begin to experience real struggles such as stress and disappointments in their lives. Could it be because they have not experienced the fullness of the power in the cycles of God and have failed to take advantage of what the Father has released to us? We all have issues in our lives, hurts and circumstances that wound and hurt us. When we go through these cycles, we have God's opportunities to be renewed. Yeshua brought the Feasts to the fullness of their meaning so that we also can experience this fullness in these appointed times.

Some people who know about the Feasts say that Yeshua fulfilled four feasts but not the Fall Feasts yet. However, from the way I see it, He fulfilled them all. In Mathew 5:17 it says: "Do not think that I came to abolish the Law or the Prophets; I did not come to abolish but to fulfill." To fulfill the writings does not mean to abolish them, it does not mean that from now on they stop from functioning. The best Hebrew word that matches the Greek for fulfill is להשלים (le-hashlim), which means to complete and to bring them to the fullness of their meaning so that we also can experience this fullness in the appointed times. There are some aspects of all the Feasts that still must take place prophetically, which I will not go into in this study. I am just focusing on how relevant the Feasts are to our lives today.

Chapter

11   One New Man

Many years ago, I studied at a well-known Bible College in the US. In one class the professor taught about the theology of the church and Israel from a Dispensational point of view. At that time, I was a very new believer and had not yet read the bible all the way through and here I was in Bible College. The professor drew charts on the board. On the first chart was Israel that received the mission from God, which they supposedly did not fulfill. Then the Messiah came and was rejected by Israel. But God did not give up and He created a new group, which is called the church.

Then the church went about the mission of God until the time it is supposed to be 'raptured' or taken out of the earth. Then for the next seven years, God turns His attention back to Israel. At the end of seven years, Israel is saved, Jesus returns, and sets up a one thousand-year kingdom where Israel dwells down here as earthly people and the church dwells above as heavenly people. The picture was complex and somewhat confusing to me. I did not understand it very well and had many questions. I waited till the class was over and I went to the professor, not to challenge him, but just to ask some troubling questions I had.

What I did not understand was how I fit into that picture because I happen to be Jewish. I said to him, "I understand that I come from this group called Israel. And now I have discovered who my Messiah is. Does that mean that I pass from one organization called Israel to another one called the church? Especially if the Messiah is the fulfillment of all the prophecies given to Israel, where would you place me in your charts?"

I could see by the reaction of this professor that no one ever asked him that question before. Because professors of that Bible College were supposed to know everything related to eschatology, he immediately cut me up and put parts of me in one place and the other parts of me in the other place.[4] I felt even more confused than before. Many, many times I went to the Lord with this question. I never wanted to stop being Jewish. I thought, as a Jew, I have my God and my Messiah. Slowly the Lord began to show me different parts of the Scripture having to do with His plan for the world.

In Genesis 28 Isaac is blessing Jacob before Jacob departs from his house. In verses 3 and 4 Isaac says, "May God Almighty *(El Shaddai)* bless you and make you fruitful and multiply you that you may be an assembly of peoples and give you the blessing of Abraham and your descendants with you, that you may inherit the land in which you are a stranger which God gave to Abraham." So the blessing is to Jacob and to his descendants. But a little earlier, Isaac says that Jacob would become an assembly of peoples, or nations. This has prophetic significance of the fact that the nations would be able to join in the blessings of Abraham.

The word for "assembly" in Hebrew is קהל *(kahal)* and this is the word that has been used to refer to the nation of Israel throughout all of the *Tenakh*, the Hebrew Bible, along with another word, עדה *(edah)*. About 2000 years ago, a very important document was produced called the *Septuagint*, the Greek translation of the *Tenakh*. In several places the word *kahal* was translated with the Greek word *ekklesia*,

---

[4] Eschatology - theology concerned with death and the final destiny of the soul and mankind.

which means called out, and the word *edah* was translated as synagogue. Israel is described by these two words, *kahal* and *edah*, both meaning assembly. *Kahal* is assembly in terms of being called out. Truly, Israel is a "called out" nation. It is not the church that is called out, but Israel. God called Abraham out of his father's house and God called Israel out of Egypt.

The word *edah* also means assembly but in terms of witness. Many Christians teach that the church began on the Day of Pentecost. When I read Acts chapter 2, I do not see that any new group that began on that day. What we see is God's amazing fulfillment of His appointed time for Israel called the Feast of Weeks (*Shavuot*). It is my understanding that the English word "church" is not a correct translation of the word *ekklesia* but something else. It was introduced to create an entity that replaced Israel. Scripturally Israel is *ekklesia* and according to the prophesy given to Jacob, it refers to the whole company of Israel – and all the people from other nations that have joined Israel by faith in the God of Abraham, Isaac and Jacob through the Messiah of Israel. Then they, too become a part of the called out of Israel.

With this in mind, let us look at John 10:15 and 16. This is Yeshua talking about Himself being a shepherd of the sheep: "As the Father knows Me and even so I know the Father and I lay down My life for the sheep." Verse 16 goes on to say, "And **other sheep** I have which are not of this fold. Them also I must bring and they will hear My voice and there will be one flock with one shepherd." So who were the original sheep and who are the other sheep? I believe the original sheep are the children of Israel, who are descendants of the twelve tribes and those who have already joined Israel over the ages, such as when a "mixed multitude went up with them" (Exodus 12:38) who travelled with Israel as they came out of Egypt. And when Israel was in Persia in the dispersion many non-Jews became Jews.

Yeshua said He came for those who are "the lost sheep of the house of Israel" (Matthew 15:24) which includes those who came from the twelve tribes as well as the strangers and foreigners who joined them over the centuries. The other sheep are people from the other nations; that is anyone who comes to Yeshua who is not necessarily born Jewish. The key here is there will be one Shepherd and one flock, not two flocks, one called Israel and one called the church.

Let us talk about some of the advantages of the Jews. Paul, whose Hebrew name was *Sha'ul*, by the way, did not change it to deny his Jewishness, it was the name non-Jews were more familiar with. He brought up a question: Do Jews have an advantage? He lists several advantages in Romans 9. They have adoption as sons and they have glory, which is the presence of God; they have all the covenants, and Torah, which includes instructions. They have priestly service and all the promises. All the forefathers came from them and finally Yeshua Himself is a Jew (Romans 9:4-5). Since we talked about covenants, who did God make a new covenant with? In Jeremiah 31, starting in verse 31 God says He would make a new covenant with the house of Israel and the house of Judah. Nobody else is mentioned.

So He did not make a new covenant with Americans, Chinese, Russians, or any other people. In Ephesians 2 when Paul is speaking to the nations that come to Yeshua, he refers to them as "you who are formally Gentiles." While they were Gentiles according to Ephesians 2:11-13 they were called "uncircumcision." Without Yeshua they were aliens to Israel's commonwealth. They were strangers to all the covenants including the new one, and without hope, and without God – they were far away.

As we continue reading Ephesians 2:19-22, we find out that those former Gentiles are no longer strangers and not called foreigners. They are now citizens with the rest of the Israelites. They become members of the household of God. This is a household that has been built on the foundation of the apostles and prophets and Yeshua

Himself who is the cornerstone of the house of God. The only covenant they could have joined is the covenant that God made with the house of Israel and the house of Judah, joined by becoming the same family. The Scriptures say we are being built together into the dwelling place of God, His holy temple.

Earlier in this book we mentioned that God wanted to build a house, which is indicated by the very first letter of Genesis. Here we can see that this house needs two parts, Israel and the rest of the people who came from the nations. The house is incomplete without one or the other. In Ephesians 3:9, Paul mentions the phrase "fellowship of the mystery". This mystery was not known in other ages and now has been revealed to the apostles and prophets (3:4). What is that mystery? That the nations could become fellow-heirs with God's people Israel. That mystery is also called in Ephesians, "A display of the manifold wisdom of God to the principalities and powers". All of this coming together, as Paul describes in Ephesians, is because it is God's heart to create "one new man" (2:15) or said another way, one new people. That is indeed a display of the incredible wisdom of God (3:10)!

According to everything that I have mentioned, it is clear to me that when people from the nations join Israel they become part of Israel with an incredible inheritance. They do not replace Israel as some people think, but they enable Israel to expand. They enrich Israel with their uniqueness. And as they join Israel they share together in the same roots and the same inheritance that Israel has from God. So what do you think people who have joined Israel become? Have they become Jews? No, they are not Jews, but they are Israel's commonwealth. They are now in and no longer out. We can actually trace the word Israel and find out in one instance where Israel is also one of the names of Yeshua Himself. In Hosea 11:1 it says, "When Israel was a child and I loved him, and out of Egypt I called My son." There is no doubt who that refers to, the children of Israel, whom God brought out of Egypt. But is there another application of that verse? In the book of Matthew, an angel appears to Joseph in a dream urging him to take the young child Yeshua and His mother and escape to be saved from King Herod. It says, "When he arose, he took the young child and his mother by night and departed for Egypt, and was there until the death of Herod, that it might be fulfilled which was spoken by the Lord through the prophet, saying, "Out of Egypt I called My Son" (2:14, 15). So Yeshua coming out of Egypt is also a fulfillment of Hosea's prophesy in the verse where the Son is called Israel. Inside the word "Israel" there is a phrase: "Prince of God" – שר אל. Yeshua is referred to by many names prophetically in Scripture and Israel is one of His names.

In many cultures, the bride will take the name of her husband. Is it alright to call the followers of Yeshua who is also called Israel, Israel? We also spoke earlier that when Abraham crossed over to God, he was called a Hebrew because that word means to cross over. In Galatians it says if you are in the Messiah you are Abraham's seed. It does not say if you are born Jewish. Is it possible, in that sense, when the people from the nations become believers in Yeshua and they cross over to God, they also become Hebrews by being grafted in? There is one more point, that the land of Israel is an inseparable part of the promise and of the Abrahamic covenant. Even if you are not Jewish, when you joined the family of God the covenants and the promises become yours. That land is now part of your inheritance whether you ever live there or not. And you must feel something in your heart when ignorant politicians want to exchange part of this land for supposed peace. They are giving away pieces of our inheritance.

There is something else worth mentioning. In Revelation it says, "And I will give power to my two witnesses, and they will prophesy one thousand two hundred and sixty days, clothed in sackcloth. These are the two olive trees and the two lamp stands standing before the God of the earth" (Revelation 11:3, 4). The prophet Zechariah had a vision of a lampstand, a *menorah*. It had two olive branches on each side of the menorah. He says, "These are the two anointed ones, who stand beside the Lord of the whole earth" (Zechariah 4:14). The way I see is that these two witnesses in Revelation are not two individuals, but as Paul mentioned in Romans 11 regarding the olive tree, they are natural branches and then the wild branches grafted into it. The natural branches are the children of Israel and the wild branches are engrafted into the same tree. Both are olive branches. It is my view that those two witnesses are Jews and the nations that have together to become one "anointed" new man. Revelation is a book that is full of symbolism. It has more symbolism than direct literal statements.

Chapter

12 The Good News

In Mark 16:15 Yeshua says to His disciples, "Go into all the world and preach the Gospel." The origin of the English word Gospel comes from the ancient English word Godspel. It is a translation of the Hebrew word that was used with the meaning of "announcement of good news". If Yeshua commands His disciples to preach the Gospel, the good news, what is it? What is the content? In the Book of Isaiah, we read, "How beautiful upon the mountains are the feet of him who brings good news, who proclaims glad tidings of good things, who proclaims salvation, who says to Zion, "Your God reigns!" (52:7). Here the good news proclaims peace, goodness, salvation, and that "Your God reigns". Obviously, the core of the message, which is being announced, is the reign or kingdom of God on the earth and not just salvation – although salvation is a part of establishment of God's rule on earth. In Mathew 24:14, Yeshua said: "This gospel of the kingdom shall be preached in the whole world as a testimony to all the nations, and then the end will come."

Why then are we given an example of prayer where part of it says, "Your kingdom come on earth as it is in heaven"? What does kingdom on earth mean to us if we think that we will spend the eternity in heaven? I will deal with these questions in a different book, but now let us return to the meaning of the phrase, "announcement of good news" and its relationship to the "flesh". The messenger of good news in that chapter is called מבשר *(mevaser)*, which comes from the verb לבשר *(levaser)*. The noun is בשורה *(besurah)* and it literally means good news as in the context of the army winning a battle, when the messenger comes first to announce the good news of the victory. When we take this verb *levaser* to the root level, the root is pronounced בשר *(basar)*. It is related to a very common noun בשר *(basar)*, which means flesh or meat. In the world of believers today, flesh usually is bad but spirit is good. A common negative expression is, "That is of the flesh". Is there a connection of "proclamation of Good News" with the concept of "flesh"? And if yes, what can we learn from it?

To find some answers we will have to go to the very beginning again, to Genesis chapters one and two. When God created the world, in the process of creation, as He finished each day, God would make a statement that it was good – כי טוב *"ki tov"* (pronounced kee tove). Except for the second day, which had no statement, every other day had a statement that it was good. In God's final act of creation, which was mankind, He made the statement, "It is very good." In Hebrew He said, טוב מאוד *"Tov meod"* (tove meh-ode).

We can see that one of the things, which becomes very clear in the creation, is the goodness of God. He creates what is good because He is good. But when we get to Genesis chapter two, after everything that was good, suddenly we read a surprising statement: "It is not good for man to be alone" (2:18). How would you like to be in the Garden of Eden, walking with God and suddenly He says: "It is not good." Does God not fill all our needs? I would say yes. But the way He created us, He created us for each other, so that we need each other in order to share together in the love that God gives us.

So God puts Adam to sleep, takes a bone out of him, forms the bone into the woman and then brings her to Adam. Adam says something really amazing. It is translated as "bone of my bones and flesh of my flesh" (2:23). The word for flesh is בשר *(basar)* and the word for bone is עצם *(etzem)*. He says, *"Etzem m'atzamai"* which does translate as bone of my bone. But the Hebrew word עצם *(etzem)* also means me, or my essence. Basically what Adam is saying is, "She is me. That is my flesh." Many rabbis say that the commandment that says you should love your neighbor as yourself does not apply to your spouse. Why? Because your spouse is you and not your neighbor.

So, how does that story end? In the next verse it says, "Therefore man shall leave his father and mother and be joined to his wife and they shall become one flesh" (:24). In Hebrew it clearly says, בשר אחד *(basar ekhad)*. That phrase, בשר אחד *(basar ekhad)*, one flesh, is the solution to that which is "not good", which is being alone, now becoming good news for Adam. So the verb to proclaim good news that comes from that very word, בשר *(basar)*, flesh, and this good news is about relationship, with Him and one another, because in Yeshua we all become one. That is the good news!

In the book of John, awesome good news is proclaimed when it says, "And *the* word became flesh" (1:14). It is the most amazing thing that the presence of God can dwell in flesh, even in our bodies, which are made out of earth. But one day "The earth will be filled with the knowledge of the glory of the Lord as the waters cover the sea" (Habakkuk 2:14). God will reign over all the earth, and His people will be one with Him as in a marriage. Maybe now you can look at the word for flesh differently and not just something negative.

I do need to mention, that when flesh is mentioned in the negative by Paul in his letters, there he is referring to the carnal mind. Flesh that is alive yet does not have the mind of God is a carnal mind. But flesh as it is presented to us by the Lord, which He created to be His dwelling place, can be a glorious thing.

Chapter

13   "Nuggets"

As I mentioned earlier, I consider these translation revelations as nuggets of gold, which are very valuable. We mentioned before that a Hebrew word is more like a picture in which we can find different pieces of the picture but when the translators translate it into another language, they have to translate a picture into a single word, loosing quite a bit. In the next couple of examples, I would like to bring up some of what has been lost in translation. I am not saying that the following passages are mistranslated, I am just saying that there is more to the meanings than the one word conveys.

Isaiah 60:1 is a very famous passage. It says, "Arise, shine; for your light has come! And the glory of the Lord has risen upon you. For behold the darkness shall cover the earth, and deep darkness the people, but the Lord will arise over you and His glory will be seen upon you." In English, the word arise is presented two times – for the people to arise and the Lord will arise over them. In English it is the same word, but in Hebrew "arise" is two words with totally different meanings.

In the first instance, the first word is קומי (*koo-mee*). It means rise. In verse 2 where it says, "the Lord will arise over you," here arise is the word זרח (zarakh). This word is what is used in terms of the rising of the sun and the shining of its light. The meaning is that as you arise, the Lord then will overshadow you with His light and glory. It is a much better picture.

Also the word קומי (koo-mee), which also means arise, is in the feminine gender. English verbs do not conjugate according to gender, so it is just translated arise. But why in Hebrew would the verb be conjugated in the feminine and not in the masculine in this case where God is addressing His people? The feminine is always about beauty. For example, Psalm 45:10 and 11 says, "Listen, O daughter, consider and incline your ear; Forget your own people also and your father's house, so the king will greatly desire your **beauty**." When God wants to address the beauty of His people, He often addresses them in the feminine. It is in quite a few places like this where the translation is entirely missed in English.

To go further with this, the next word in Isaiah 60:1 takes us even further. This word is translated as shine and in Hebrew it is אורי (or-ee). That word can be actually translated two different ways. If you translate it as a verb then the correct translation is shine. But that verb can also be treated as a noun. In that case, the translation will be, "my light." We would then translate the verse as "Arise my light, for your light has come." In other words, the Father is saying, "You are My light, and I am your light." Or simply said in Hebrew, oree (my light), orech (your light).

There might be some scholars who would argue over which is correct, but to me, knowing that every Hebrew word is a greater picture, it is not one or the other, but both. What I see in that sentence, where it says, "Arise my light, and shine, for your light has come" it is saying, "Shine, for YHWH, who is your light, has come."

Since we are in Isaiah, let us look at chapter 53, which contains some very well-known verses. For one, "He was wounded for our transgressions, He was bruised for our iniquities. The chastisement for our peace was upon Him, and by His stripes we are healed" (53:5). The word for stripes is translated from the Hebrew word חבורתו (havurato). The singular word *havurah* has several meanings. One of them is wound, and another is joining together or having fellowship. So the passage can also be translated, by His fellowship, or friendship we are healed. I believe these are the same Hebrew words and that both meanings are in there. The wound and the fellowship are intertwined, because Yeshua said, in John 15:13, "Greater love has no one than this, than to lay down his life for his friends." His wounds are tied to His fellowship with us.

There is another Scripture that says, "Faithful are the wounds of a friend" (Proverbs 27:6). This word in Hebrew paints a bigger picture of our Special Friend who was willing to take our pains upon Himself and be wounded on our behalf. This concept cannot be translated adequately with just one word. Yeshua offered Himself on our behalf. In the *Tanakh*, there were many offerings that were a type of what He would later fulfill. When we talk about different offerings that are mentioned in the book of Leviticus (*Vayeekrah*), one of them is called the "burnt offering." In Hebrew it is mentioned only by one word, עולה (olah). This is spelled with the Hebrew letters, *ayin*, *lamed*, *hey*. This is not the Spanish word *hola*, but it comes from the Hebrew verb עלה (a-lah), which means to ascend. When the Israelites would bring a sacrifice to God where the whole animal was burned, and the smoke went up to heaven, it is called *olah*, because of the rising up or ascending of the smoke. The altar for this sacrifice had no steps to it, but rather a ramp. This symbolizes that He causes us to "ascend" when we come before Him with the blood of the offering.

Earlier we mentioned that the Torah through many symbols describes God's people as elevated. For example, God elevated Israel out of Egypt. Every time anyone goes to Jerusalem, they go up, and always go down when they leave. With this in mind, it is important to mention another verse, Deuteronomy 28:1: "Now it shall come to pass, if you listen diligently to the voice of YHWH your God, to do carefully all His commandments which I command you today, that YHWH, your God, will set you on high above all the nations of the earth."

In Hebrew, the status of high above is described by the word עליון (elyon). That word often refers to God Himself, which means The Most High God. God does not mind describing his people, whom He elevated, as being high where He is. Since עלה (alah) is part of the sacrifices, it is also worth mentioning that the word for sacrifice in Hebrew, which is קרבן (korban), and to sacrifice is להקריב (le-ha-kreev) which comes from the root קרב (karav). From the same root another word can be derived which means close. So the Hebrew word sacrifice really means to draw near or to come close. It is about our closeness with Him. Because of Yeshua's sacrifice we experience closeness with God.

Chapter

14 More Nuggets

As we come toward the end of this book, I wish to give you a few more instances of where understanding the Hebrew will bring you a greater and more realistic understanding of certain passages. In Genesis 4 and 5 there is a genealogy beginning with Adam's son Seth. If we put all the nine names in these chapters together they actually tell a story. As we have said before, Biblical names have meanings that often reflect the character and identity of the people.

The first name would be Seth, *Set* in Hebrew, and his name means appointed. Set has a son whose name is Enosh (Eh-nosh), which means man in the sense of being mortal and frail. Enosh has a son whose name is *Kenan* (Kay-nan). It means owner or possessor. *Kenan* has a son who was named *Mahalalel* (Ma-ha-la-lel), which means praiser of God. If we stop here and look at these Scriptures, it would seem that these four names describe an appointed man who is a possessor and a praiser of God.

Mahalalel has a son whose name is Jared in English, in Hebrew *Yered* which means to come down. So this appointed man who praises God comes down. The next son is *Hanoch*, which is Enoch in English. His name means dedicated or consecrated. So the appointed praising man who came down is dedicated. Enoch's son's name is Methusaleh, in Hebrew *Metushalach*. This name has two words: to die and to send. So the name means sent to die. It is interesting that the man who lived the longest has a name that means was sent to die.

So this appointed man who came down and praised God was dedicated and was sent to die. The next son is Lamech, *Lemekh* in Hebrew, which means poor, made low. Now this man that was sent to die was made low, was humble. The next and last son in this genealogy is Noah, in Hebrew *Noakh*, which means rest. This appointed man, a possessor and praiser of God, came down, was consecrated and dedicated to God. He was sent to die, and by humbling Himself He brought rest. Can you see the prophetic significance of these names, which God hid for us to search out? Do you recognize who this man is?

Anyone who has read the story of Abraham and Sarah knows that they received a promise to have a child, but it took many years of waiting before Sarah conceived and gave birth. Truly this was a supernatural fulfillment of the promise because Sarah was way past the child-bearing age. In Genesis 21:6, after Isaac was born, as we read in the NKJV, Sarah said, "God has made me laugh and all who hear will laugh with me." In Hebrew the name Isaac is יצחק (*Yitzhak*), which literally means he will laugh. The way the sentence reads in Hebrew is, "And Sarah said, God had made for me laughter צחק (*tzhok*), and everyone who hears about it, will laugh יצחק (*Yitzhak*) with me." Isaac is *Yitzhak* and laughter is *Tzhok*. The deeper meaning is that God gave to Sarah Isaac whose name means laughter, the promised miracle son and everyone who learns of it and laughs with Sarah takes part in that miracle.

Matthew 4:17 tells us of Yeshua's early message. It says, "From that time, Yeshua began to preach and to say, 'Repent for the Kingdom of God is at hand.'" In Matthew 11:12, He said something that often presents variations in interpretations of this verse. He said, "From the days of John the Baptist until now, the Kingdom of heaven suffers violence, and the violent take it by force." In Luke 16:16 it says it a bit differently. It says, "The Law and the prophets were until John. Since that time the kingdom of God has been preached and everyone is pressing into it." So Matthew says "take it by force", while Luke says, "Everyone is pressing into it."

In reality when we study the Greek words in both, "suffers violence" or "take it by violence", the Greek words are actually equivalent to the Hebrew word פרץ (paratz), which means to break out, to burst out or to breach. If we look in Genesis 28:14 we will see how this verb is used. It is a promise of God to Jacob, "Your descendants will also be like the dust of the earth, and you will **spread out** to the west and to the east and to the north and to the south; and in you and in your descendants shall all the families of the earth be blessed." Where is says "spread out" is that very word פרץ (paratz). So really God is saying, "Your seed will break out in all four directions."

Micah 2:12-13 says, "I will surely assemble all of you, O Jacob. I will gather the remnant of Israel. I will put them together like sheep of the flocks, like a flock in the midst of their pasture…. The one who breaks open will come up before them; they will break out, pass through the gate and go out by it. Their king will pass before them, with the Lord at their head." It is very much worth giving our attention to these two verses. Where it speaks of the remnant of Israel, the remnant in this verse is related to sheep in a fold. The next verse says that the one who breaks open, or the breaker, which in Hebrew is פורץ (poretz), had gone before them so that the sheep broke forth and crossed over and came out. It is saying that the King will go before them with YHWH at their head.

When we go back to the phrase, "The kingdom of God suffers violence", we need to understand that at the foundation of the sentence is this breaking in. The meaning here is that the Kingdom of God broke in, and as the Kingdom of God broke into the fold, now the sheep, that is the people or remnant, are breaking out into freedom. In other words, they have been set free. That verse has nothing to do with attacking or storming the kingdom. Yeshua's audience would have understood what He was referring to.

What has been translated as violence is really the breaking in of the kingdom to the sheep. The kingdom of God breaking in is really Yeshua coming and He is the breaker who sets the sheep free. When He appeared on earth, it was a beginning of the breaking in of the kingdom of God on the earth. That is why His main message is, "The Kingdom of God is at hand." It is not just a future event. It is like He was saying that which Israel had been looking forward to for so long was now finally here.

John 10 also paints a very similar picture. It says, "...He who enters by the door is the shepherd of the sheep, to Him the doorkeeper opens, and the sheep hear his voice, and he calls his own sheep by name and leads them out. And when he brings out his own sheep, he goes before them, and the sheep follow him, for they know his voice" (10:2-4). We can see that the shepherd of the sheep enters into the sheepfold and leads the sheep out. The sheep are the lost sheep of the house of Israel because in Matthew 15:24, Yeshua said, "I was not sent except to the lost sheep of the House of Israel." But a few verses down, the Lord is speaking of the other sheep that are not of this fold. They will also hear His voice and together they will be one flock with one shepherd. The other sheep, I believe, refer to people from other nations that will follow the king of Israel (Yeshua).

In Psalm 84:1 where it says, "How lovely is your tabernacle", in Hebrew it means, "How friendly are your dwelling places." In Hebrew it is in the plural meaning of many dwelling places, not just one tabernacle location. When we worship and praise God in the Spirit, there are realms of the Spirit so that wherever we encounter God in the Spirit we are in His dwelling place.

Psalm 89:7 says, "God is greatly to be feared in the assembly of the saints, and to be held in reverence by all those around Him." When you look at the meanings of a few words, rather than, "God is greatly to be feared", in Hebrew it says, "God is majestic in the counsel of the saints, and awesome upon all those around Him." When you look at the context of this Psalm, it is not just about fearing God but the focus is that He is majestic. It is about who He is – awesome and majestic!

CONCLUSION

In reading through this book, you have taken a journey into an amazing world that has been hidden for a couple of thousand years, at least from the time that Hebrew ceased to be a spoken language. I want to encourage you, if you do not know this language, do not feel like you are obligated to learn Hebrew. What gives us true life is the life of the Spirit. An exciting walk with God is a walk of learning and revelation. Because of that, my intent was to mine some nuggets of Hebraic biblical understanding to encourage you in this walk of discovery.

In Proverbs 25:2 it says, "It is the glory of the Lord to conceal a matter, but it is the glory of kings to search out a matter." We can easily say it is having the heart of a king to search out a Biblical matter. In Hebrew the word for matter is דבר (*davar*). A good explanation of the word *davar* is reality. Everything that God created is *davar*. And He created it by *davar*, by His word. That means that whenever we discover something it has already come from His word. It is interesting to me to see that God hides things, not *from* us, but *for* us to discover. Children love to discover things. To me discovering is part of the process of walking with God as His children.

It is not about gaining more information. I do not believe we will ever know everything. If we come to a place where we would know everything, then there is nowhere left to go. And that spells death to me. That is why when Moses asked God about His name, the answer was, "I will be what I will be" and not "I am who I am." It is so important that it is in the future tense, and is ongoing. Yet as we walk with God He allows us to discover things that we need in any given moment or to overcome obstacles that might be set before us at any time. He is with us always in the future and right now! And there is always more to learn about Him.

I wish you all the blessings from the Father as you continue your walk of discovery. Whatever things, small or big, they are treasures from heaven that God releases into your life as gifts of His love and His goodness toward you. May you have total success in Him, in every area of your life – like Joseph, in the Book of Genesis. He was called "a successful man", in Hebrew איש מצליח *(ish matzliakh)*. He was successful in every area of his life. May you also be *ish matzliakh*.

ABOUT THE AUTHOR

ALYOSHA RYABINOV

Alyosha was born in the city of Kiev, Ukraine. His family was comprised of very gifted and serious classical musicians for generations. His grandfather was a composer and violinist; his father was a violinist and conductor in the Kiev Radio Symphony Orchestra; and his mother is a classical guitarist who authored books on classical guitars and teaches in universities and gives private lessons in Chicago, Illinois.

As a third-generation professional musician, Alyosha's childhood consisted of a rigorous and disciplined upbringing. In addition to his academic courses, he simultaneously studied composition with one of the leading composers in the Ukraine. By the age of fourteen, he was already composing operas and symphonies.

Alyosha immigrated to the USA in 1979, where he completed his Master's Degree in Piano Performance and Composition at DePaul University in Chicago. He is a world-class composer and concert pianist. Many international doors have opened up to release a new sound in music worldwide, which is often accompanied by glorious healings to his audiences.

He has published over a dozen CDs. This music reaches deep into the listener's heart and spirit, as it is known to transport his listeners into new heavenly dimensions of God's love and deep peace. Though there are no words in much of Alyosha's music, words are often heard in people's hearts and visions, and revelations are often received. Out of His Jewish background, Alyosha releases ancient Hebraic blessings during every concert. Many report how their hearts and bodies are healed at every concert and also in events where he teaches along with his music.

Today Alyosha teaches on many topics from the original Hebrew text. He links both the *Tenach* (Older Covenant) with the New Covenant Scriptures and makes them come alive. His most effective topic to teach is how to move beyond religion and to experience one's faith as a living reality in their heart, resulting in changed lives and relationships!

Jody Ryabinov, Alyosha's wife, most often joins him in sharing the reality of the love of God. She also holds an informed knowledge of health and how the body heals, which often contributes to imparting wisdom and discernment regarding healing.

From 2010 Alyosha and Jody permanently live in Israel.

To obtain Mr. Ryabinov's books and music, visit his website at www.SongofIsrael.com or email him at info@SongofIsrael.com.

Lightning Source UK Ltd.
Milton Keynes UK
UKHW020638011119
352727UK00012B/1230/P